URBAN BUMPKINS

URBAN BUMPKINS

ROBERT MANKOFF

ST MARTIN'S/MAREK

Of the one hundred and twenty-two cartoons in *Urban Bumpkins,*
81 appeared in *The New Yorker*, 13 appeared in *National Lampoon,*
8 appeared in *Saturday Review,* 5 appeared in *Psychology Today,* and
15 were previously unpublished. If you can tell which are which, you
may have a future ahead of you as a magazine editor.

Library of Congress Cataloging in Publication Data

Mankoff, Robert.
    Urban bumpkins.

    1. American wit and humor, Pictorial.   I. Title.
NC1429.M358A4 1984   741.5′973   84–22904
ISBN 0-312-83430-6

First Edition
10 9 8 7 6 5 4 3 2 1

Dedicated to _____
(YOUR NAME)

Robert Mankoff was born a long time ago in a place far away called The Bronx. It was a different Bronx then, bucolic, with lovely Flora and Fauna and their ugly stepmother Gloria as well. A few years later he and his family moved to the Lower East Side.

Then as today the Lower East Side was a haven for the small entrepreneur. Every day Bob's father would set forth with his pushcart laden with stacks of cartoons and every evening he and the laden pushcart would return. "The bastards want to laugh but they don't want to pay for it," he would say in his heavily unaccented English. Bob's mother, surveying the wreckage that a life devoted to laughter had wrought, would say to him, "Fido (her pet name for him), don't grow up to be a humor monger like your father." "But Mom," he would growl, "I was born with a gift for laughter and a sense that the world is mad." "So be a garbageman then," she said. "Really, you want me to be a garbageman?" he asked. "As long as you're the *best* garbageman" was her answer. But that proved impossible in a city of eleven thousand sanitation workers. The highest he ever placed was 738th.

Flushed with disappointment, Bob's thoughts returned to cartooning. His father's naive approach had failed. He had worked hard but what did he have to show for it? An entire couch made out of unsold cartoons. If Bob followed in his father's footsteps he'd soon have a couch of his own. The trick was not to work harder than his father, but smarter.

Accordingly, he enrolled in the College of Cartoon Knowledge. The school was steeped in the academic tradition of cartooning. The entire first year was spent drawing desert islands from detailed reproductions of plaster casts that Daumier himself had used. Not until the second year were students flown out to real desert islands for life drawing. Bob had breezed through those first two years but the third year proved his undoing. He dropped out, unable to handle the physics, calculus, and organic chemistry that had mysteriously appeared on the curriculum.

Now Bob was back to square one but, lo and behold, this wasn't the same old square one. It was no longer filled with losers and has-beens but with upscale achievers who just couldn't afford the outrageous rents on squares two, three, four, and five. Yes, square one had been gentrified and its sides were now dotted by condos, boutiques, and singles bars. What's more, this trendy enclave now sported four local papers: *The North Side News, The East Side Examiner, The South Side Sentinel,* and *The West Side Watchdog,* all of which proved eager markets for Bob's zany, serious, broad, subtle, timeless, topical, hilarious, lugubrious humor, which you can now enjoy merely by turning these pages.

URBAN BUMPKINS

"You're not my husband."   *"Please, I've had a hard day."*

"I know it doesn't look that great now, but once you accessorize it with the right jewelry, I guarantee you the whole 'Mr. T.' look will fall into place."

"Three tones will follow. Then there will be some buzzing noises, a woman giggling, and the incomparable Louis Armstrong singing 'I'll be glad when you're dead, you rascal you.' The woman giggling marks the correct time."

MANKOFF

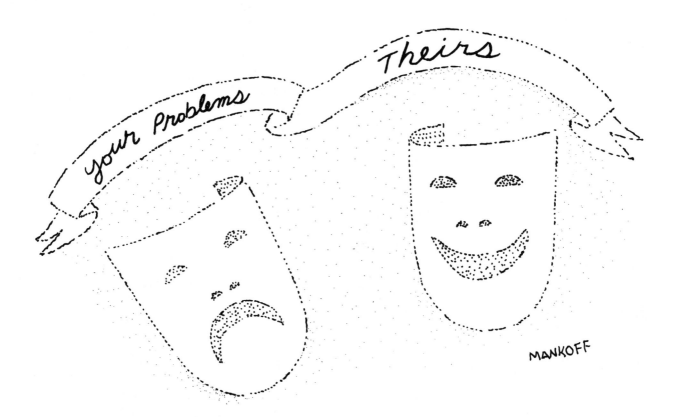

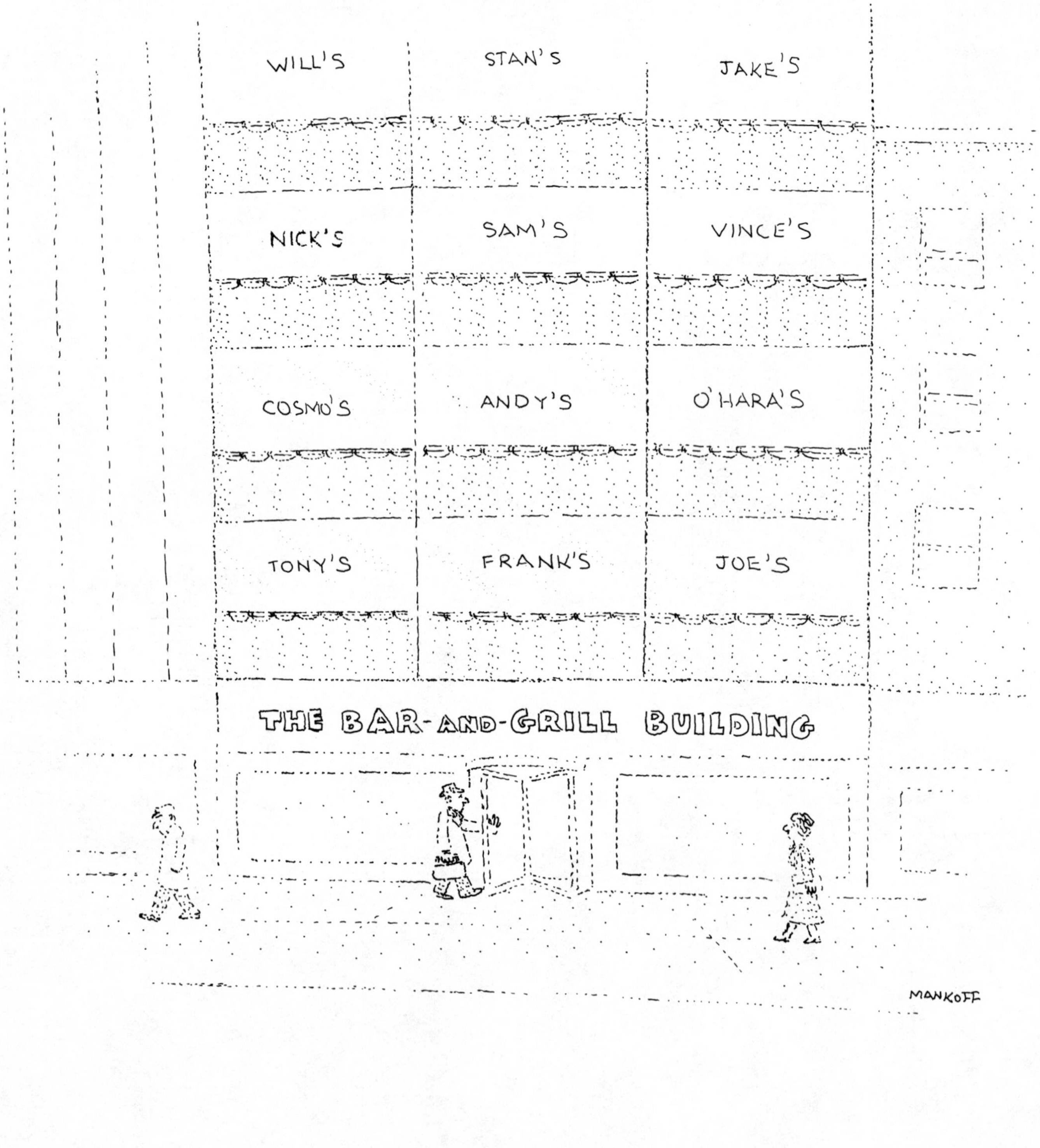
WILL'S
STAN'S
JAKE'S
NICK'S
SAM'S
VINCE'S
COSMO'S
ANDY'S
O'HARA'S
TONY'S
FRANK'S
JOE'S
THE BAR-AND-GRILL BUILDING
MANKOFF

"Personally, I'd have preferred more transit cops."

From left to right: Albert Hartley.

"Sorry, full."

MANKOFF

*"O.K., but change 'Her tawny body glistened beneath the azure sky'
to 'National problems demand national solutions.'"*

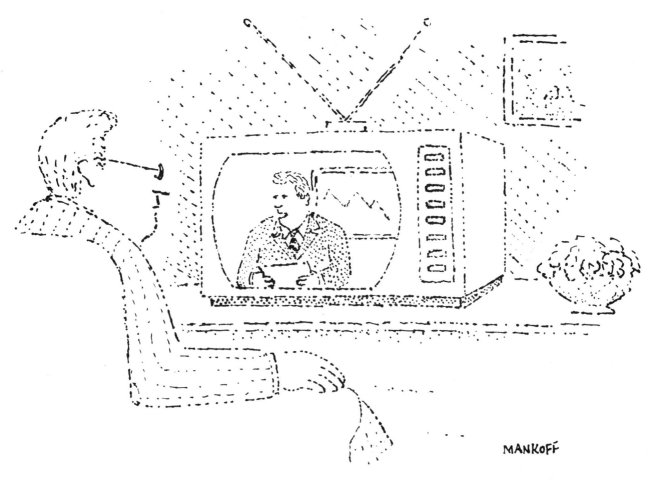

"On Wall Street today, news of lower interest rates sent the stock market up, but then the expectation that these rates would be inflationary sent the market down, until the realization that lower rates might stimulate the sluggish economy pushed the market up, before it ultimately went down on fears that an overheated economy would lead to a reimposition of higher interest rates."

Three Out of Four Doctors

"Gersten, how do you think you'd perform in a zero-gravity environment?"

"And for my next act I will escape from a galvanized-iron can filled with water and secured by massive locks."

"I don't mean to stir anything up, dear, but don't you think that perhaps our divorce was a little too amicable?"

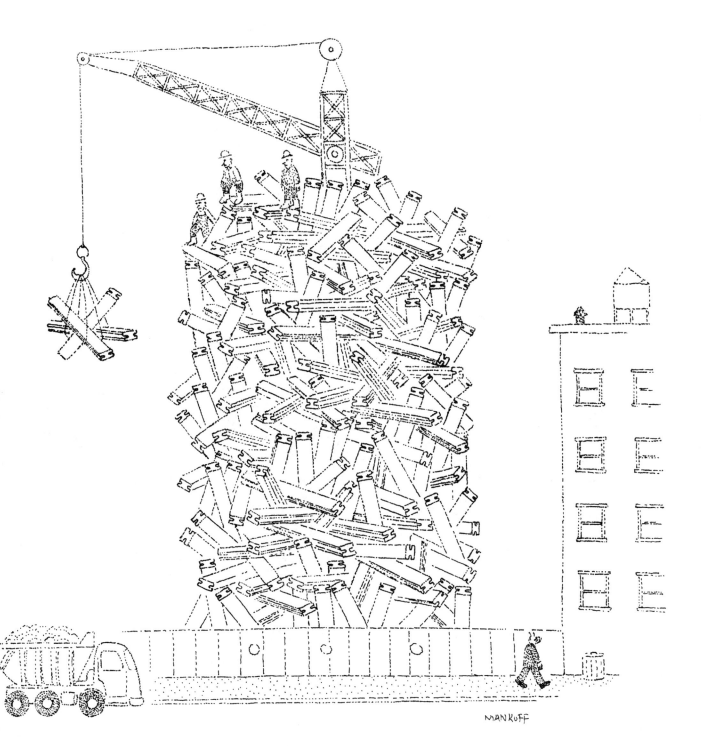

"And you, Al, what would you do if you had only a million?"

"'Scuse me, Officer, but where do the elite meet to eat around here?"

Savory Types

"We lost all our traveler's checks!"   *"That's too bad. What kind were they?"*

"Fine Al, and how are you, your charming wife, Joni; your two wonderful children, Charles and Lisa, ages thirteen and fifteen; and your delightful German short-haired pointer, Avondale?"

"Well, so long, Bert."

"Now, this over here, this is why you're going to have to go to jail."

"Stick with your breaking stuff. Your fastball's lost its credibility."

"None for me, thanks."

"Don't you think 'Workers of the world, unite! You have nothing to lose but your chains' will send the wrong signal to the financial community?"

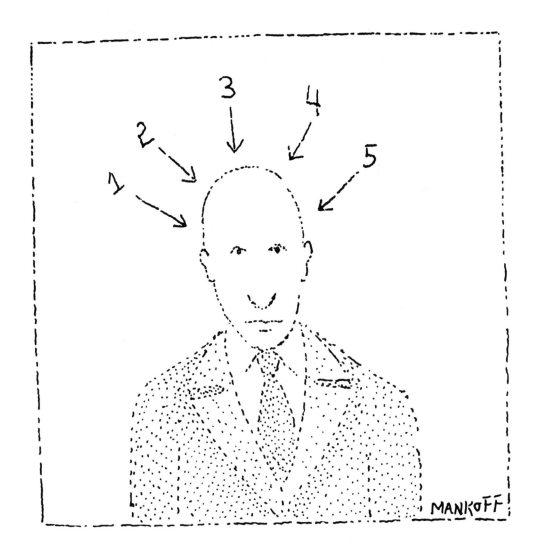

The Five Major Warning
Signs of Baldness

"Hi. We're all members of the eighteen-to-thirty-four-year-old age group that you're a member of. Come out and play with us."

"Seasonal enough for you, sir?"

"F train coming, Kimosabe—two mebbe three stops away."

"Maybe they're not the only factor, but I believe the Soviets are an important factor in the destabilization of our marriage."

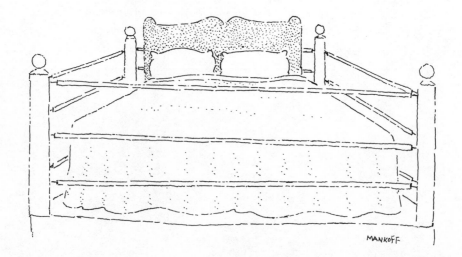

"If birds fly over the rainbow, Garber, why, oh why, can't I?"

"The boys in research seem to think it has something to do with aerodynamics, Chief."

"*Jake, what's the word that means wood suitable for building houses, ships, etcetera, whether cut or still in the form of trees but in this context is taken as a warning that a cut tree is about to fall?*"

"You were found sleeping in your car in the middle of the day. How do you plead to the charge of impersonating a police officer?"

"Somehow, this isn't how I imagined it."

"One last question, Berlinger. Is it just you, or is the whole damn Accounting Department shot full of steroids?"

MANKOFF

"Did he say the budget was going to be a zillion billion krillion dollars or a krillion billion zillion dollars?"

INTERMISSION

AND NOW BACK TO OUR BOOK

HIGH-TECH COMEDY

MANKOFF

MANKOFF

"And now I'd like to sing a little song written specially for me called 'I Wanna Be President.'"

Suddenly a delightful Continental custom is sweeping America!

MANKOFF

"All right! Have it your own way. It was a ball."

MANKOFF

*"Well, Phil, after years of vague complaints and imaginary ailments,
we finally have something to work with."*

"He has some final words he wants to say, Nurse. Send in his speechwriters."

"Good as far as it goes. Now let's see if you sound like Claude Rains."

Zack Brillard and Live-In Companion

"Well, so long, Jeff, and give my regards to the little woman you're living with."

Author's Query

For an autobiography of the journalist, wit, author, and amnesiac
Harlane Sedgwick, I would greatly appreciate any information.
—Harlane Sedgwick

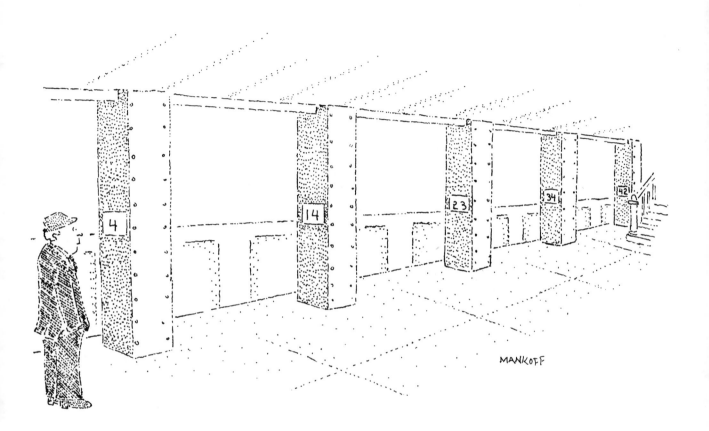

"Let's look at the facts, Stienfeld: daily newspaper circulation is lagging behind population growth, gas was first used in 1915 to break the trench warfare stalemate, the cassava is fast becoming one of the world's most important tubers, and finally, for God's sake, Stienfeld, apes have nails not claws!"

Secretary of Comedy meeting with other Cabinet members.

"That wasn't very nurturing of you."

"The arithmetic seems correct yet I find myself haunted by the idea that the basic axioms on which the arithmetic is based might give rise to contradictions which would then invalidate these computations."

"Will the owner of the car with license 417–JHL please move it?"

Comprehensive, Authoritative, Washable

ENCYCLOPEDIA VALENCIA

MANKOFF

"Brilliant! The marines will be here before you know it."

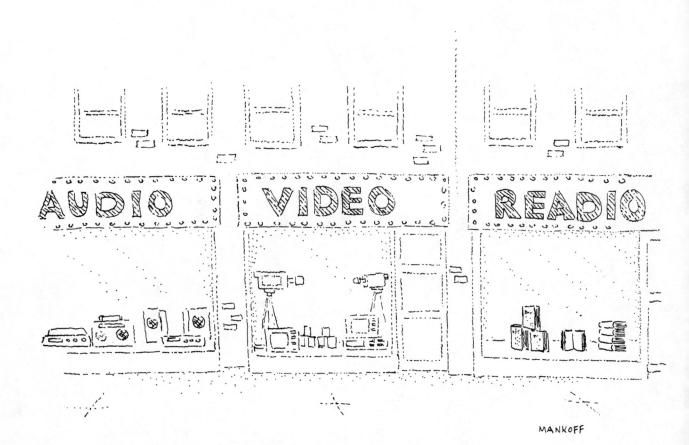

MANKOFF

"Sorry, sir, you'll have to hang on some more, but I'm going to advance you to priority-hold status."

"Hi. You two wrestle, don't you?"

The Man of a Thousand Faces

No. 687

"*Look, maybe you're right, but for the sake of argument let's assume you're wrong and drop it.*"

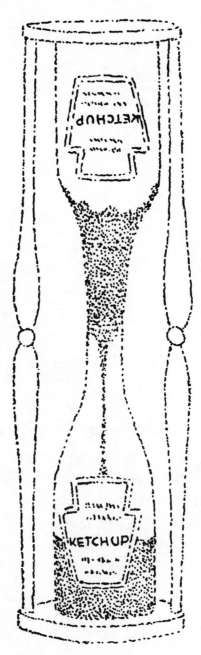

MANKOFF

Look, Joel, you're relatively young, have a relatively nice job and a relatively nice wife. There's no reason in the world why you shouldn't be relatively happy."

HE SHOULD KNOW.
STILL, TAKING THE ADVICE OF A FISH COULD GET YOU COMMITTED.
COME ON IN! THE WATER'S FINE!
MANKOFF

*"Harold doesn't ordinarily care for the Muppets, but tonight's guest
is Paul Volcker."*

"I'm looking for something that expresses the spirit of the season but doesn't neglect the need for a credible deterrent."

"I've given him your message. Please have a seat. He'll be out with his hands up in a minute."

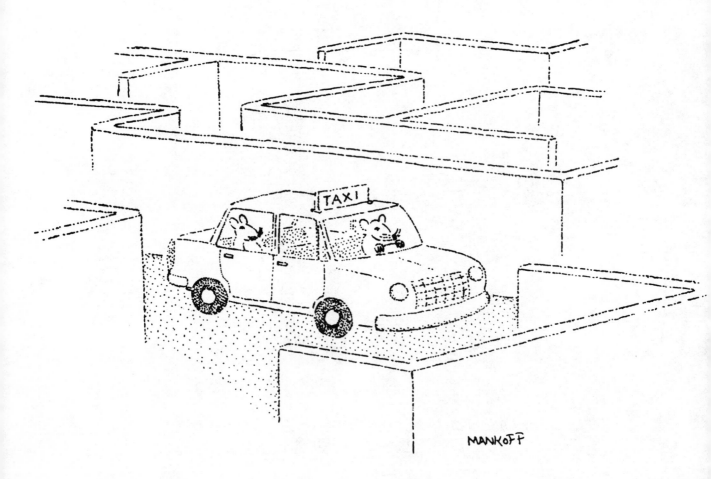

"That was very nice, dear, but don't you think you should begin to address yourself to a broader constituency?"

"Watch ya back! Watch ya back!"

EFFECTS OF THE ENVIRONMENT

IDENTICAL TWINS SEPARATED AT BIRTH.

"The people's response to your proposal has been mixed. The majority of the mail is favorable but the rest are letter bombs."

"What a day! First the car almost stalls going out of the driveway. Then my pen runs out of ink at work. And now I'm having some trouble opening this button on my coat."

A No-Nonsense Guy with His No-Nonsense Wife and Their No-Nonsense Dog

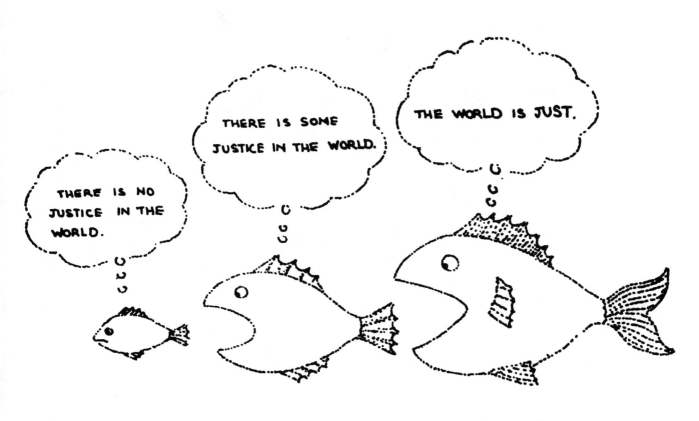

"*Look, I'm an optimist. I believe that the concerted action of government, business, and labor under the leadership of a strong President can slow the rate at which the country is deteriorating.*"

MANKOFF

"Good work, Bevans, but in this business climate I've got to ask myself the question 'Is a choreography department absolutely essential?'"

CONDOMANIA

"Edgar, you've been retired for three years now. Why don't you loosen your tie?"

"No, I'm sorry I can't. The time function seems to be broken. But you
might be interested to know that November 2, 2006, falls on a
Tuesday."

"My point, Dad, is that however this list of who's been naughty and who's been nice has been obtained, it represents an immoral invasion of privacy, and makes whoever compiled it especially ill suited to sit in judgment over the ethical behavior of others. And incidentally, the part about checking it twice just adds insult to injury."

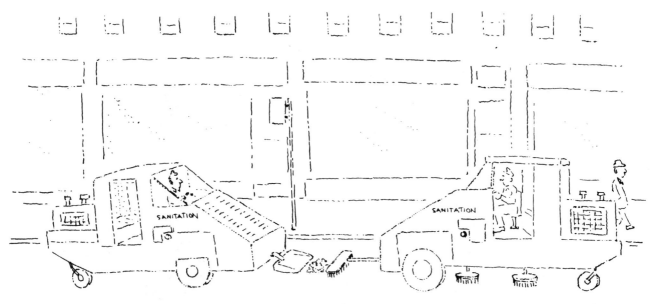

THE TOO PERSONAL COMPUTER

"Miss Braverman, bring in everything we've got on long division."